THE SHE CHRONICLES
History's Maverick Women

Poems by

Lisa Rodgers

First published 2015 by IRON Press
5 Marden Terrace
Cullercoats
North Shields
NE30 4PD
tel/fax +44(0)191 2531901
ironpress@blueyonder.co.uk
www.ironpress.co.uk

ISBN 978-0-9931245-1-8
Printed by Ingram/Lightning Source

Copyright © Lisa Rodgers 2015
Cover design by Brian Grogan
Book design and layout by Brian Grogan and Peter Mortimer

Cover portrait of Mary Robinson

Typeset in Georgia
IRON Press books are distributed by Central Books
and represented by Inpress Ltd
Churchill House, 12 Mosley Street,
Newcastle upon Tyne, NE1 1DE
tel: +44(0)191 2308104
www.inpressbooks.co.uk

Contents

Introduction ... 5

Mary Shelley:
i. Mother ... 9
ii. Widow ... 10

Anne Bonny: Pirate ... 12

Dido Belle:
i. Mulatto ... 14
ii. Lady ... 15

Mary Robinson:
i. Flirt ... 17
ii. Spurned ... 18
iii. Girlfriend ... 19
iv. Witness ... 20

Sally Salisbury: Inmate ... 22

Hannah Snell: Soldier ... 24

Aphra Behn:
i. Traveller ... 26
ii. Spy ... 27
iii. Playwright ... 28

Mary Wollstonecraft:
i. Rival ... 30
ii. Deserted ... 31
iii. Revolutionary ... 32

Fanny Burney:
i. Dreamer ... 34
ii. Watcher ... 35
iii. Companion ... 36

Margaret, Duchess of Newcastle:
i. Barren ... 38
ii. Maverick ... 39

Theroigne: Activist ... 41

Lady Mary Wortley Montague:
i. Bather ... 42
ii. Cougar ... 43
iii. Forgotten ... 44

Duchess of Devonshire: Celebrity ... 47

Image credits ... 48

Author Biography ... 49

Introduction

The poems in this collection are inspired by the courageous, unconventional, pioneering and indomitable spirits of some remarkable Restoration and 18th century women. Their histories and accomplishments are mostly absent in the modern consciousness and were invariably ignored or belittled in their own time. The women are disparate with regard to class and personal circumstance, however they are united by their audacity in being unconventional, or even simply notable, at a time when this was the prerogative of men.

These poems are not works of historical fiction. Just as observations and reflections on contemporary life and experiences are harnessed as poetic material, so some impressionistic gleaning of the lives ahead provided the muse for this collection. And while many are necessarily flavoured with historical nuance, there is a universality in what the lives of these extraordinary women present to us: as individuals who know what it is to hope, love, struggle and survive.

Lisa Rodgers

For my darling girls, Stella and Daisy

Mary Shelley

Mary Shelley (nee Godwin, 1797 - 1851). Mary was the daughter of notable philosopher parents: William Godwin and Mary Wollstonecraft. Her mother died a week after giving birth to her due to complications resulting in septicaemia. Aged 17, she absconded with the poet Percy Shelley, travelling around Europe with him and bearing four children, only one of whom survived. Mary was widowed at the age of 24, Shelly having drowned in the Gulf of Spezia. She was a successful novelist, most notably the author of the gothic novel 'Frankenstein', as well as an editor, critic, travel writer and literary historian.

Mary Shelley
i. Mother

You put lightning into my hands
And said it would save her.
As you pushed us off into the Grand Canal
I pleaded with empty blistered palms.
But you were a Bauta mask of neutrality,
Stood between my sister and your club-footed hero.
You had done your bit.

You were not there
When I shaded her eyes from the leer of the thick-tongued grotesques,
When I traced droplets of fever into a cross on her brow.
You were not there
When I traded my youth for one more day with the stone Christ of the sea bed,
When I lullabied the water coffin into a cradle of ever afters.

Amongst the porticos I looked for him,
The doctor from Ingolstadt
With the Lazarus sparks in his fingertips.
But he was floating face down
Under the Bridge of Sighs
From where a hunchback,
With dull yellow eyes and a stitched face,
Took mice from his pocket
And hung them
As a prescient warning to all travellers.

Mary Shelley
ii. Widow

I place offerings at the feet of Teshub:
Curls of our lost children's hair;
The last cries of my mother's labour;
Your barnacled heart.
He prods at the pile with his bloodied mace and leaves with a shrug,
Spitting out bird bones.

I am faded now, and cowed.
I dare not look the summer moon in the eye
For fear her beauty will seduce me to hope, again.

It is the villagers who tell me of your fiery ascent,
Of the catafalque of drift wood,
Your second drowning in oil, frankincense and salt;
The flames' aura melting you into a watery shroud.

The mourners fight over your spoils, the cleverest one
Claiming your skull for a drinking cup.

And for me? I have frozen every word you have written
Into the ice bath that saved me.

Anne Bonny

Anne Bonny (1700–1782) – a notorious pirate, operating in the Caribbean. Bonny's family moved from Ireland to the New World when she was a young girl. She began mingling with pirates in the local taverns in the Bahamas where she met, and later married, the pirate 'Calico Jack'. They were joined at sea by a handsome new mercenary who eventually revealed herself as Mary Read. Together, they plundered dozens of merchant vessels along the coast of Jamaica.

Anne Bonny
To Mary Read

Pirate

There was no mistaking you,
Though you tried to drown
Your beauty in a frown,
Swore to swagger over your poise,
To salt your arias to the gulls.
I could see the lightness in you.

I saw you weep when the turtle's
Blood moaned about your feet.
When a lashing took an eye,
Your stare searched the dumb horizon for pity.
When you reeled, giddy in the yardarms,
I watched your delight escape in rips of cloud.

I will keep your secret
Until I no longer love you:
When the sepulchral call of the midnight whales
Has stolen your charity,
And the dominion of fist and foot
Sits like a cockroach at the corner of your smile.

Dido Belle

Dido Belle (1761-1804) Born to a distinguished British naval officer and an enslaved African woman, Dido Bello was brought up as a gentlewoman at Kenwood House, England, home to her great uncle, William Murray, 1st Earl of Mansfield and Lord Chief Justice. Dido, famously painted with her cousin in a portrait by Johann Zoffany, lived at Kenwood for 30 years until after Murray's death and her marriage to Frenchman, John Davinier.

Dido Belle
i. Mulatto

I was birthed between a barrel and a bitt,
Sluiced out onto the deck with only the cook as witness,
Gathering up his second best ladle and pot-hook.

My mother cried out to the stone eyes of the night,
Blinking into a darkness heavy with memory:
I was hers for as long as now would last.

She laid me on her torn, linen osnaburg,
Marvelling at the blankness of my skin,
Tracing her fingers over the absence of a branding.

Below deck, the Captain stirred molasses into his rum,
And while black shark fins circled the ship,
He raised a silent toast to my screams.

Dido Belle

ii. Lady

Would it have been easier
If I'd entered the room
In a milk-maid's apron,
Flecks of cream winking from these dusky cheeks?

Or perhaps your shock came not from
The ostrich feather in my hair or the emeralds at my throat,
But from my assured smile
And insistence on holding your stare.

You will assume I am something bought
To impress, like the Turkish rugs or the Sevres china,
Or that I have used my arts
To bewitch this childless pair.

I advise you to be careful:
Do not look too long at the wool of my hair
Or drop your chin when the Master takes my arm.
Look at this place – I am untouchable.

Mary Robinson

Mary Robinson (née Darby, 1757?–1800). Mary became an actress on the London stage when her husband's debts threatened to ruin the family. She earned her nickname «Perdita» for her role as Shakespeare's heroine in The Winter's Tale in 1779. Her beauty and charm won her the attentions of the then Prince of Wales and she became his mistress for a time. Struck down with a debilitating illness when she was 26, she re-invented herself as a best-selling author, poet and feminist thinker.

Mary Robinson
i. Flirt

The hosts are drunk.
Aurora is whispering into Comus' ear,
Her dress straps fallen,
Her hand squeezing his arm.
He rises and re-fills her glass.
This is Eden's autumn
With every lit tallow
A virtue spent.

I sit in my brown Quaker gown
Daring watchers to lust for irony.
I shall play Pamela and run from Mr. B
(After chaining my ankles to the table).

The 'wicked Lord' beats my husband at Ombre
Toasting his opponent's horns
While he smoothes the silk
Over my five months belly.

As I waltz around the shrunken prodigy's harpsichord,
I happily throw steaks of propriety
To the wolves in the gallery.
All my gold is on red.

Mary Robinson
ii. Spurned

You tried to end it with a note:
Five words scratched over the thousands you wooed with.
You had it delivered to the willow tree,
Hoping, no doubt, its weight would snap
The branch that held me.

But this 'lost one' is not sunk.
She is gathering fistfuls of rue
To bake into an eel pie for you,
Lined with promises, bonds of faith
And your "Je ne change qu'en mourant" paper heart.

I have invited some guests to our Hell House:
A few gossip columnists; your father with his whip;
Your latest bandy-legged bitch; and my friend Sheridan
To remind you that you have neither the nobility of soul, or the looks,
To ever play the Dane.

Mary Robinson
iii. Girlfriend

Touching up your lipstick, I stall breath,
Mirror-mouthing a cushioned 'O',
Shakily tracing the rise of your kiss.

We stay up gambling until three,
Removing pearls to cover our losses,
Demanding another game from the blurred sycophants.

Your husband frowns from the doorway,
A tumble of gasping rabbits slung from his shoulder-
Ironic, you say, considering his own reluctance to mate.

I see in the soup terrine that my pouf
Has slumped to the left, and nods at
The rake who burnt my initials into his lawn.

You fall off your chair and the spinning stops.
Hitting away help, your place is resumed
With a hiccup and an orange-girl's laugh.

Let us fill our glasses and retire.
And in the morning, sack your servants.
I do not like them; they have no envy in their eyes.

Mary Robinson
iv. Witness

They spewed you out of the boat –
An inconvenient Noah, left to mouth forgiveness into the sand.
When your fish-flesh started to harden
They clothed you in a sail and left.
So much depends on pity.

No-one claimed you, not even the tide.
I wished you away, troubled by the
Animation of your hair in the wind
And the pointing of your left hand.
By the second day you would ruin this view forever.

My joints ached at the thought of you -
Feet, clod-swollen and blue -
Fingers, calcified and crabbed around
The grey goose feather that tried
To write you into myth.

When the arguments were finally over
You were dragged to higher ground
And buried under a pile of stones.
Some nights, when your cries pierce my sleep,
I sit by your side and sing lullabies,
Not out of kindness, but as penance.

Sally Salisbury

Sally Salisbury (c.1692–1724) – a celebrated prostitute in early 18th-century London. She was celebrated for her beauty and wit and attracted many aristocratic customers. Aged nine, she ran away and lived on the streets of the slum district of St Giles, living a life of petty crime. In 1723 she stabbed and wounded a client in a dispute in a tavern in Covent Garden. She was sent to Newgate Prison to serve her sentence but died there after only nine months.

Sally Salisbury
Inmate

I thought I would die laughing
When they pushed the old cow down the hill in a barrel.
Even when they cut off that French tailor's nose
Round the back of the Opera, I had a giggle.

Reputation is everything, they say.
It does not matter whether it is
Earned or invented,
It must be got and kept at any price.

I lost mine down the Three Tuns last month;
Fixed a bread knife into my Finchy's chest.
Thought he was looking at another girl you see,
My sister to be precise. Gave her a quick slashing too.

He forgave me there and then
As his pretty blood spread across his shirt
Like a tide dragging him under.
He asked for a surgeon, not a watchman.

What makes a woman like me?
It is not the Ratafia or the Usquebaugh tea-
Although my breath is almond sour
And I often share the Mohock's pipe.

I am Need, ungoverned.
The sweet-faced poor girl,
Scraped out, punched and paraded
Until half a crown for one hour of love becomes a Duke's fortune.

I would not thank you for your pity;
I have a better life than you.
Whores and bastards make their own luck.

Hannah Snell

Hannah Snell (1723–1792) When her husband deserted her, Hannah borrowed a suit from her brother-in-law, James Gray, assumed his name and joined the navy. For over two years she concealed her true sex, sailing to India and fighting at the Siege of Pondicherry where she was wounded in battle. After her petition of the Duke of Cumberland, she received a lifetime army pension from the Royal Chelsea Hospital.

Hannah Snell
Soldier

I defy the logic of you.

Nuzzled into my lap
You play fate's paramour
Shortening my breath
With your rough fidelity.

Did you see me
As an easy conquest
With my pallid cheeks
And slender wrists?

Thought I would submit
To your baneful purpose
With the obedience of a spaniel's throat
Beneath his master's boot?

I have sharpened a whale bone
To surprise your complacent bed
Of throb and burn,
And I will dig for you
With the fervour of the chained:

My life is light against my freedom.

Aphra Behn

Aphra Behn (1640–1689) An English Restoration dramatist, widely credited with being one of the first women to earn a living by writing, her most notable works being the play 'The Rover' and novel 'Oroonoco'. She was also thought to have travelled to South America and the Low Countries working as a spy for Charles II. Behn lost her income when the king refused to pay her expenses and turned to writing for the London Theatre to make money. Almost entirely self-educated, she was often mocked by critics for her lack of classical knowledge.

Aphra Behn
i. Traveller

The parrots lied.

I am laid out on sacks of coffee beans
Under a burnt sky that has taken many bribes from opportunity.
Quick fingers untie my bonnet
Which is passed from hand to nod amongst the crowd.
The gold show of my hair falls to gasps,
Its theatre belying the truth of its dank, infested roots.
Behind my closed lids, the spinning compass -
Which has been my companion for the past four months -
Persuades me that, if death is close, I should not fight him off.
I surrender to the loosening of my rings, my garters, my laces.

The chatter of my welcoming party is hushed by
A pair of dark arms.
As they lift me, I trace the earthworm belly of scars
Which bracelet the rise of muscle.
My nose is nipped and my chin raised.
I open, a defiant maw of freckles and powder,
As a bitter liquid froths at my vanity.
A rough hand clamps my mouth and I sway
With the resignation of a hunted marmoset
Shackled to a stick.

My lids flicker.
Through the tobacco smoke, a procession of cargo creaks
Along the jetty:
Rug columns, bearded portraits, filigree bird cages.
Down at my feet, a camel-flye rests on my ankle and takes root,
Flowing with my veins down into the mud.
My wake is abandoned.
I will live.

In the shadow of a gallows, I open my right hand;
Splinters of amber glass pierce my palm.

Aphra Behn
ii. Spy

You pulled away from the body parts,
Laid out and labelled for ease of reference:
Digby's liver; Rookwood's brain; Fawkes' heart;
But laughed as Janklaassen drove his truncheon into Katrijn's head.

I stare at you through my monocle
But you fold into a mountebank's promise.
You said we could be ourselves here,
Flanked by the menageries and the marionettes.

I pick at the scab you cut into my arm:
160 4 159 – our covers blown, ciphers laid bare, for love, you said.
But all the time your Siamese head looks over your shoulder,
Nodding to the King with your warrant in his fist.

In this light, your profile reminds me how, last night,
I allowed my eyes to reflect you, just for a blink.
Now the Fool enters stage left and performs a
Headstand into a bucket of water until the laughing stops.

Ah Will, here is my billet-doux of betrayal,
Written in lemon juice, just as you like it.

Aphra Behn
iii. Playwright

The curtain rises to reveal me caged, suspended,
Mutinous arms and legs flailing through bars,
Clawing at the air like a river dipped witch.
This did not happen in rehearsals.

From out of the wings strides my cod-pieced understudy,
Delivering a Prologue of apologies and regrets
That bursts my nose with betrayal.

Spitting out orange peel, I tear through pages of script,
Searching for the true beginning
Where I seduce with wit in my breeches.
I am too soon.

Buckingham sharpens his quill on my ambition
And scrawls: 'Poet or Punk?' on my forehead.
Mr. Pepys tuts disapproval as he fumbles in his neighbour's petticoats.
Ms. Gwyn applauds from the King's lap, her swollen belly chinking with sovereigns.

The curtain falls as Fop Corner chants an Epilogue in Latin.
I understand only "meretrix".

Mary Wollstonecraft

Mary Wollstonecraft (1759–1797) A writer and philosopher, Mary wrote 'A Vindication of the Rights of Women' arguing for equality of education and opportunity for women. She spent time in Paris during the Revolution and wrote a history of its beginnings. Mary had several difficult and fraught romantic relationships, being abandoned by the father of her first child. She eventually married the esteemed philosopher, William Godwin, but died a week after giving birth to their daughter, Mary.

Mary Wollstonecraft
i. Rival

Through the keyhole
I watch you:
Propped up and pretty
Amongst certainties of silk.
You tease the noses of puppies
With capricious fingers
Which admonish and forgive.
You do not hear
The peasant fiddler
Weeping at his Caoineadh,
Heeling out a rhythm
To soothe the dead
On your dumb boards.

I have the key
To the nursery.
I feed your children sugars of devotion
When they wail
Into your absence.
I loathe your husband
With his pitch-capped morality
And the choke of
His gun-powdered dreams.
But I enjoy
His interest in how
I slide the queen
Across your chess board.

I am the surprise
Beauty in the bog –
With a spade-cleft smile,
My skin leathered by disappointment-
Confounding an old maid's fortune,
Coming for your name.

Mary Wollstonecraft
ii. Deserted

The one true thing
Is a fish head
Caught in the reeds,
Its vermillion eye
Reflecting the bridge.

Mary Wollstonecraft
iii. Revolutionary

Church bells collude with red sky cries.
The promise of breeches and bread
Is bartered for God's handprints on a purple coat.

A giant carries the king above the crowd
Along an avenue of pulsing bullocks' hearts.
The Prince asks, "Is it still yesterday?"

The queen bribes her spyglass to lie –
To frame short sight as generosity
And burn the rope from the marionette's neck.

Fanny Burney

Fanny Burney (1752–1840) – a celebrated novelist and letter writer, Fanny's first novel, Evelina, published anonymously in 1778, took London by storm. When her identity was revealed, Burney's debut into literary society was launched by the fashionable hostess Mrs. Thrale through whom she met and became great friends with Dr. Johnson. She published three further novels to great acclaim and is thought of by many to have influenced the writings of Jane Austen.

Fanny Burney
i. Dreamer

Dear Nobody,
They say I shall remain small,
Lilliput legs forever dangling mid-stool
Like a regretted promise.

I scribble against this prognosis,
Dragging letters into a new order
In defiance of a dish-cloth destiny.

Sisters,
Your breathing charms my midnight candle,
Possesses the feathers of my quill
But this little dunce will scratch her own fame.

I pick at my needlework scars
Beneath what Newton called *his* stars.
They find me mumbling like a fire's first flush.

When I ashed my last pile of chattels under the frosted oak
They all thought I was saved,
That reputation was restored along with my appetite.

They did not know it was paper I chewed,
Dabbing the ink from my lips
With a blue stocking.

Fanny Burney
ii. Watcher

I take my seat at the turn of the stairs,
Forehead lined against the spindles,
Framing the chatter and chink.

The dark foreigner is my favourite, bowed up in Manchester velvet
Looking between guests and nodding at nothing.
He picks up a fork that a servant drops and offers it back,
Meeting surprise with a frown.

The soprano, La Bastardina, rests her hand next to his lace cuffs,
Eyes lidding lust at his accidental touch.
Her companion elbows disapproval, jabbing a fork into her silver ribs-
A reminder of the debt she still owes.

The Russian Empress's lover heads the table
Picking myths and prophesies out of his oyster shell teeth.
He spins Yekaterina's portrait in an open locket,
Blurring her face into a flickering sneer.

And then there is second Mama,
Striking a match to start a bonfire of my juvenilia.
Her laughter flatters like a tailors' gasp and flutter clap.
I enjoy the sagging of her plucked chin over throttles of pearls.

Only Mr. Garrick senses me. He winks up at my shadow.
I remember how once he sailed me to the Isle of Dogs
And let me be Miranda to his Prospero.
I would have spurned any Ferdinand to stay.

Fanny Burney
iii. Companion

I am your pet.
Curled up next to you on Mrs. Thrale's couch,
You feed me morsels of meat
Which I will later regurgitate.

I have learned to greet your shakes and twitches
With the nonchalance of youth;
I can look at the purple of your scars
With a total lack of discernment.
And so you love me,
Soothed by the conviction of my art.

The Queen, apparently, was not so mannered
When your cold abscess was offered for her touch;
Her reported wince fed your melancholy for years.

But here, you are you,
As you charm and pontificate
And I sift through the shale of your clucks and whistles
To hold the beauty of your words
Up to the light.

Margaret, Duchess of Newcastle

Margaret, Duchess of Newcastle (nee Lucas, 1623–1673) an aristocrat, writer and scientist. Unable to have children she embarked on a life of study and engagement with ideas. She published under her own name at a time when most women writers published anonymously. Her writing addressed a number of topics, including gender, power, manners, scientific method, and philosophy. Because of her defiance of expected female mores and her unconventional dress, Margaret was viewed by many as mad, but not by her husband.

Margaret, Duchess of Newcastle
i. Barren

On the first day of bleeding: take a lettuce that has run to seed,
Finely chop, boil for one hour and drink the liquid until sunset.
On the second day: add two spoons of pale wine to two spoons of tansy,
Drink morning and night for 10 days.
Following this: mix two spoons of red sage with the urine of a pregnant sow,
Drink daily for as long as is needed.
If, after eight weeks, you are still not blessed,
Consume powdered sex organ of either boar or stag
As often as supply allows.
Alternatively, combine the blood of a hare with the left hind paw of a weasel,
Mix with vinegar and swallow during the first hour of every third dusk.

It is essential for success, to restrict mental activity of any kind
As this saps energy and obedience from the womb.
Pray for forgiveness of previous sins and all activities
Offensive and unnatural to your sex, such as promiscuity and learning.

Make gold out of stone.

Margaret, Duchess of Newcastle

ii. Maverick

Can you feel my heart through the wall?
It is reaching for you: kissing your brow;
Whispering at your temple; watching from your shoulder.
In you I am me.

Later, you will look at my scribbles
And smile, nodding your wisdom
At creatures without blood, liquors that burn out disease,
Rivers in the sun, age-purging oils distilled from desert rocks.

You will buy me a microscope and soothe
My horror at the giant louse and killer flea.
You will instruct the scientists to substitute
The frog or mouse in the vacuum to spare my tears.

And when the arsworms mock my 'antik' dress and 'peculiar singularity'
You will hide their pamphlets of scorn.
And I will be your Penelope.

Anne-Josèphe Théroigne de Méricourt

Anne-Josèphe Théroigne de Méricourt (1762/9–1817) – an activist during the French Revolution. She campaigned for female equality in politics and education. Whilst speaking in the Tuilerie Gardens in Paris in June 1793 she was violently attacked by a group of more radical female revolutionaries. She subsequently suffered severe headaches and episodes of erratic behaviour and was confined to an asylum for the rest of her life.

Theroigne
Activist

Don't frighten the birds.
You are frightening the birds.
It is alright my dears,
Do not be afraid;
They will not harm you.
It is me they want.
Fly from their stones.

Who is this?
Hide.
Ah, brother, it is you.
Let me rest my broken cheek
Against your shoulder
And we will talk of liberty.

La femme a le droit de monter sur l'echafraud;
Elle doit avoir egalement celui de monter a la Tribune.

Beware the harpy's tongue.
It must be stopped.
Cut out the hope or we are all lost.

Keep still.
Lie flat on the ground.
Whisper into the earth;
It will cloak you until they are gone.

I have a saviour hiding in the sewers.
Look how his skin blisters and cracks
But his heart is pure.

Pass me the water;
The Tuilerie dust embalms my feet.

Lady Mary Wortley Montague

Lady Mary Wortley Montagu (1689–1762) – an English aristocrat and writer, well known in polite and intellectual society for her wit and verse. As wife to the British ambassador, Lady Mary chronicled her experiences in Turkey through her 'Embassy letters'. Her social circles included some of the most noted thinkers and writers of the day, including novelist Henry Fielding and poet Alexander Pope. In middle age she fell in love with the young Italian author Francesco Algarotti and spent most of the rest of her life living and travelling in Europe.

Lady Mary Wortley Montague
i. Bather

Under a dome of lights
I trade my coat for skin.
The women put a bird
Inside my corset
And weep for my imprisonment.

Steamed air embroiders our brows
With shivered, democratic drops.
They serve me coffee in
Soucoupes of silver gilt
And whisper "uzelle, pek uzelle"
While anointing me with amber.

Titian has not been here;
These forms ridicule his slovenly strokes.
And Mr. Pope:
We can see your stunted shadow
Through the gauze.
Beware the precision of bodkins.

Lady Mary Wortley Montagu
ii. Cougar

I fear growing wise above all things
As judgement and propriety would
Deny the perfection of our
Interlocking fingers
And scorn the
Quickening of my breath.

There is no map
To guide the lover.
I am lost in a mist
Which veils all lines,
And rusts to a stop
Time-piece hands.

When you are gone
I trap your name in jars.
By their firefly glow
I weave your hair
Into a tapestry,
Wounding the white hart
With shards of youth.

Lady Mary Wortley Montagu

iii. Forgotten

Through the rain I search for you
Counting back the cobbles to your feet.
I side-step the cracked ones in a staccato dance,
Cheating the runes of Dido.

The letters I wrote you are in
The hands of beggars:
They shake their heads at hope
And burn my words for warmth.

Your magnificence has ruined me.
The flatterers pull at my sleeves
But your loss blurs the outside
With an abscessed insistence.

The portrait you left with
Has disappointed us both:
My offering of desire
Balded and scarred by distance.

But my pockets are too small for stones,
And my humour too light,
So I wait here, and write:
Only poetry is truth.

Georgiana Cavendish

Georgiana Cavendish, Duchess of Devonshire (7 June 1757–30 March 1806), was a leading member of late Georgian society, famous for her extrovert personality, her trend-setting fashions and her championing of the Whig party led by Charles James Fox. She lived for many years in a notorious "ménage à trois" with her husband and his mistress, and had an affair with the future prime minister, Charles Grey, which almost ruined her.

Duchess of Devonshire
Celebrity

I no longer keen when I smell another woman on my husband's hair;
I store retribution in vials of poison for his dogs.

Alone in the garden, I push my palms into rose thorns;
The whispering blood soothes like promises.

Sometimes my lungs are afraid of the horizon;
They dare not rise against their cage for fear they offend.

My friends eat mirrors and lies;
They hollow out integrity with a crested spoon.

Reporters hide in my conscience;
Their inked beaks scratch out tomorrows with a death warrants'
flourish.

Laudanum steals my days with a thirsty jealousy,
Furtively gathering up blessings into her smoking skirts.

My placenta leaks possibility; it is as weak as my will.
Babies are baptised in a flush of claret and tears.

I love a woman with a touch-piece smile;
In her I float on childhood seas that drown expectation and remorse
with each sigh of the tired moon.

Image credits

Aphra Behn (née Johnson) © National Portrait Gallery, London
Artist: John Riley

Anne Bonny (b.1697) and Mary Read (coloured engraving), American School, (18th century), Private Collection, Peter Newark Historical Pictures, Bridgeman Images

Frances d'Arblay ('Fanny Burney') © National Portrait Gallery, London. Artist: Edward Francisco Burney

Margaret Cavendish, Duchess of Newcastle (1624-74) (engraving), English School, (17th century), Private Collection, Bridgeman Images

Theroigne de Mericourt, c.1789 (oil on canvas), French School, (18th century), Musee de la Ville de Paris, Musee Carnavalet, Paris, France, Archives Charmet, Bridgeman Images

Lady Mary Wortley Montagu © National Portrait Gallery, London
Artist: Christian Friedrich Zincke

Sarah Pridden, alias Sally Salisbury (engraving), English School, (19th century), Private Collection, © Look and Learn, Elgar Collection, Bridgeman Images

Mrs Robinson (oil on canvas) Reynolds, Sir Joshua (1723-92) (after), Laing Art Gallery, Newcastle-upon-Tyne, UK, Bridgeman Images

Hannah Snell © National Portrait Gallery, London
Artist: Richard Phelps

Mary Shelley © National Portrait Gallery, London
Artist: Richard Rothwell

Georgina Spencer, Duchess of Devonshire. Private Collection, Photo © Liszt Collection, Bridgeman Images

Mary Wollstonecraft © National Portrait Gallery, London
Artist: John Opie

Lisa Rodgers

LISA RODGERS was inspired by an unconventional English teacher at the age of 14, kindling a love of literature that would influence her primary passions and her future. She moved away from her native Newcastle to study literature at university, subsequently training as an English teacher; she has spent most of her adult life trying to instil an affection for the written word in the next generation. Lisa currently lives a few streets from the sea in Whitley Bay.
For *The She Chronicles*, her first published collection, the author combines her interest in history, biography and the female experience to evoke the voices of some remarkable, yet often marginalised, Restoration and 18th century women.

We publish only a handful of titles each year, but we try to make them special. Look at our website to see what we do: www.ironpress.co.uk

Below are a few examples of recent IRON Press books:

THE PALE HANDBAG OF THE APOCALYPSE
by Eileen Jones
We are excited to introduce a distinctive new voice in female poetry. Eileen Jones' first full collection *The Pale Handbag of the Apocalypse* is technically accomplished and full of intelligent wit, skewering the absurdities of modern life. The poems work with a highly distinctive and sometimes satirical or surreal humour.
PRICE £8.00

LIMEHAVEN
Poems by Vicky Arthurs
This evocative collection of poems in inspired by memories of the eponymous home of the poet's grandparents.
As Vicky Arthurs writes in her introduction.
Their home was a haven, their garden a place of wonder and discovery........ I learned the names of things and rolled them round my tongue. They had special words I never heard at home — barometer, antimacassar, chrysanthemum, forty winks. They seemed to me exotic — as lovely and perfumed as the roses bulging beyond the lattice window.
PRICE £8.00

THINKING ONCE A WEEK
Haiku by Colin Stewart Jones
We are among the leading haiku publishers in the country. Colin Stewart Jones' miniature book leads us through a year in the poet's life, with a haiku for every week, spanning the natural world, city life and personal relationships.
PRICE £5.00

Lightning Source UK Ltd.
Milton Keynes UK
UKOW04f2310260515

252337UK00002B/37/P